Fault Lines

Fault Lines

Tim Hunt

The Backwaters Press

Also by Tim Hunt

Scholarly Works

The Selected Poetry of Robinson Jeffers, Stanford University Press 2001.

The Collected Poetry of Robinson Jeffers: Volume Five: Commentar and Critical Apparatus, Stanford University Press, 2001.

The Collected Poetry of Robinson Jeffers: Volume Four: Poetry 1903-1920, Prose, and Unpublished Writings, Stanford University Press, 2000.

Kerouac's Crooked Road: Development of a Fiction, University of California Press, 1996.

The Collected Poetry of Robinson Jeffers: Volume Three, 1938-62, Stanford University Press, 1991.

The Collected Poetry of Robinson Jeffers: Volume Two, 1928-38, Stanford University Press, 1989.

The Collected Poetry of Robinson Jeffers: Volume One, 1920-28, Stanford University Press, 1988.

Poetry

Lake County Diamond, Intertext Books, 1986.

Published by: The Backwaters Press
                  Greg Kosmicki, Rich Wyatt, Editors
                  3502 North 52nd Street
                  Omaha, Nebraska 68104-3506
                  thebackwaterspress@gmail.com
                  http://www.thebackwaterspress.com

                  ISBN: 978-1-935218-16-6

Acknowledgments

Grateful acknowledgment is made to the editors of the magazines in which the following poems (some in earlier versions) first appeared:

Alehouse: "Red Light (Salt Lake City, 1976)"
The Azorian Express: "At Dusk/Sonoma County" (material
    incorporated into "Sonoma Coast")
Cloudbank: "Stories"
Coal Hill Review: "After Listening to Art Tatum Play Piano"
Cut Bank: "F.S.A.: Fleeing a Dust Storm"
Eleventh Muse: "The Day After the 100th Anniversary of the '06
    San Francisco Quake"
Epoch: "Billboard (Middletown, California, 1962)" (as "The Map")
Fourth River: "Eucalyptus" (forthcoming)
Glass: A Journal of Poetry: "Canned Tuna" and "Car Radio
    When It Seemed Late at Night (Gunsmoke)"
Grasslimb: "High Desert, Noon, Early Fall," "Home Again,"
    "Night Shift, First Death," and "Train Window"
High Plains Review: Part 2 of "First Memory" (as "First
    Memory")
ISLE: "The Language of Light," "Sonoma Coast (Three Scenes),"
    "California Foothills," "High Desert (Three Scenes)," and
    "Early Winter (Pacific Northwest)"
Montana Review: Part 1 of "First Memory" (as "Morning Call
    Café")
Natural Bridge: "1955"and "Plate Glass (Sebastopol, California)"
Paddlefish: "When the Back Steps Seemed Very High"
    (forthcoming)
Quarterly West: "Why the Land Is Red (Lake County, California)"
Rat's Ass Review: "Grace Wilson Rouke" (Part 2 of "Absence")
    and "Levi 501s"
Rhino: "Mackinaw Parade, 2004"
Southern Poetry Review: "The Web" (as "Stories")
Spillway: "Fault Lines" and "Corn Field with Trees (Central
    Illinois)"
Spoon River Poetry Review: "Soft Shoe"
Tar River Poetry: "Passing Through: Nevada Night," Part I of
    "Absence" (as Part 2 of "Addition"), and "The Summer

She Was Seventeen (1947)"
Westigan Review: "Middletown, California" (as "Rattlesnake
    Season")
Windfall: "After the Festival to Honor the Poets: Robinson
    Jeffers and William Everson"

"Lake County Elegy" was the first prize poem in the 1983
Chester H. Jones competition and appeared in the competition
anthology that year. "Star Thistle," "Lake County Diamond,"
and an earlier version of "Stories" first appeared in the chapbook
Lake County Diamond (Intertext Books). "Cornfield with Trees
(Central Illinois)" and "Mackinaw Parade, 2004" are based on
photographs by Ken Kashian and each are included in his
collection *The Mackinaw River Project: Photographs by Ken
Kashian.* I would like to thank John Balaban for his advice on
an earlier version of this collection. I would also like to thank,
especially, Betty Adcock for her generosity of spirit and her
thoughtful encouragement when it was needed most.

Fault Lines

Prescript (Poetry)

1

2

3

4

About the Poet

for Susan

Prescript (Poetry)

for Leslie Wykoff

"How clear," my friend asks,
"is it okay to be?"

Do you remember
waiting for the yellow bus

standing a bit apart
from the others

the muddied water
of the puddle

gleaming through
a skin of morning ice.

That's how clear.

1

California Coast (Sonoma County)

The swaybacked barn,
like the eucalyptus,
seems always
to have been here—
weathering
to the grain of stone,
trailing its fence
like an old thought
across the hill.

*

The dye
marking the backs
of the market lambs
is the brown
of dried blood.

They have cropped
the headland so bare
the hills glow

in the late sun—
knuckles of a fist
gripping the water.

*

Below, the fog
on the beach
is already
heavy as sleep.

Against the still
clear sky
a gull
tunes the darkening.

Train Window

From the train, the clothes
lines and empty fields
are a motion, far away—
as if in black and white.

Then, through the rain-spattered glass
someone is riding alongside, a bicycle—
a second motion falling slowly back,
and we are here, now.

The rain gives these gifts,
unwrapping the red
and yellow branches
to open the passing ravine,

where a pickup
noseless like a rusted skull
gleams in the skin of water.

The Language of Light

for John when he was four, and now again

Here, the light in summer is so absolute
everything blooms dust.
But now it is as if the land
is willing to be seen—
miles of sage and black rock
instead of miles of light.

Each season has its own texture
—a thumbprint we learn
without noticing but know, instantly,
even after years away: north Pacific coast,
upstate New York, Utah, Maine,
each place has spoken light.

Do you remember the morning you came in
from playing in the dirt of the yard,
as all small boys do, to explain that something
was "not when it's golden light with the long
shadows, but bright light"? That
is the language of light.

Corn Field with Trees (Central Illinois)

In late fall the trees line each
side of the road
as if the asphalt furrow
were a creek
drawing the roots.

All summer they have listened to the corn
whispering as the stalks
scraped and grew.
Now the bared branches interweave
against the light—like hands talking.

It is the sky's turn to listen.

(after Ken Kashian's photograph
"Anchor Trees, Late Fall 2003")

Red Light (Salt Lake City, 1976)

At 1ˢᵗ South and Temple, a parking lot prairie,
an Indian in a blanket coat inhales
deeply from a jug of glue.

He leans back, spinning
from the lamppost, a war lance,
as the high clouds drift.

Then the cowboy, skinny in a Levi jacket
and pointed boots, takes his hit—
drawing the jug from the hip
quick, hard like a gun.

At their feet the gutter's broken glass
spikes like cacti and the prairie dog cans
watch them hug and shuffle the uneven
circle of the West they've won.

California Foothills

At night the hills pull back so far
we plant our houses against the nearest ridge,
draw the shades, and turn
to the lamp's weak pool of light.

It is not the dark we fear
but the distance it reveals,
moon and stars, the tree at the field's edge—
each distinct in the absence of the day's
clutter, the busy strands
that weave us into the moment.

On this night if we ventured out
we would find the moon so dark
that the house shutters are like the cataracts
on the old woman's eyes.

Inside she is knitting
wide braids of needles and wool.

Early Morning from a Hotel Window

Long Beach, California

Across the empty parking lot,
the new aquarium's curved wall
is an ocean painted beneath
a painted sky: blue on blue green.

Staged against the harbor's masts
and scrim of clouds: a whale
swims over a passing car,
kelp floats from the sidewalk.

But what tells us, even at a glance,
that this is not water and sky
are the way the colors never quite
catch the light they mime.

        How care-
        fully we are
            tuned—
        light and eye—
        to these
            vibrations
        and demand
            their tuning,
        even as our world
            ceases
        to be leaves and sky.

High Desert Valley (Summer, The White Mountains, California)

1

At first light the boulders
on the ridge above the ranch
are each a precise gray.
As the day builds they
will fade into auras
of heat. But at this moment
they are rocks, and the light
is still light.

2 (driving, noon)

Riding the rising thermals
a hawk drifts across the valley,
dips and arcs back.

The interwoven nerves
of the field mice etch
each pass of the shadow—
like a seismograph
sensing the distant
twistings of rock.

This time I could stop,
walk into the brittled sage
and wait for the heat
to make me its own.

But I would still not be
calibrated to the rock's
dance, or the flinch into the stillness
deeper than fear.

3

At dusk the still bright dust quiets
the glare, and the eye can see
the light that rims the western ridge.
Behind the house the one telephone wire
runs on low poles along the alfalfa field.
It whispers in the cooling air,
another shadow that speaks of night.

Leavings (Cattle Ranch, High Desert, Eastern California)

1 (Leaving)

The bed of the sand scraped truck
is a tangle of hay hooks, black
baling twine, and barb wire.

I have come back to the ranch
for my half of the leavings—the books
I won't reread, a chipped
coffee mug someone gave me,
and the memories it seems
I will have to take as well.

I am talking to the ranch manager,
each of us leaning on the truck
looking into the tangled bed—as if posed
for some TV commercial for
worn trucks that always run so buy
the shiny new one, or cheap beer
and mountains of clean snow
with horses kicking sprays of powder.

He knows I have come back
for my half of the leavings;
he's done this before, both
his part and mine, and so
we talk, carefully, past
the things the script says "leave out,"
as if here, in this high desert,
only the light can be clear, direct.

Soon it will be time to leave;
he jokes about all my "stuff,"
then shrugs and tells me of LeRoy
who walked out across the cattle guard
to the county road wearing an embroidered
shirt, his good saddle on his shoulder, and said
"Wear the best; burn the rest."

2 (Later, Another Leaving)

Smart, tough, he loved that desert
right down to the ticks and up
to the high cow meadows—a cow man,
the tiny feet and big, hard belly,
and the dog he loved better than his wife,
though he loved her too,
until all those amber shells of glass,
the slowing eye, and the morning's
shaking hand proved him right at last:
dog and desert.

Masks (Berkeley, California)

On Telegraph the aging children
sit against the bookshops and café walls,
their hands extended as if in prayer.

And when the eyes look up, the eyes
are the smoked glass of a burnt fuse.
That is why we look away and walk on.

It is not the begging or shame
at the passive need. It is the eyes—
the emptiness behind the smear of ash.

There are reasons to hurry, reasons
to believe it matters where we are going.

After the Festival to Honor the Poets, Robinson Jeffers and William Everson

for Rob Kafka

That weekend Everson was still alive, but stooped
like a question mark, rail thin and quavering
with Parkinson's, even as the spirit continued
to rebel against the once sweet flesh.

That day we honored Jeffers, long dead, and this
last time his self-proclaimed disciple—
as if Carmel were not a gauntlet of boutiques
and their years of work might buy us belonging.

Now, as the plane climbs over San Francisco,
the ocean fog piles against the city's western edge.
Behind the ridge of low hills the bay is still
clear, the bridge shining against the dark water.

By itself this would be beautiful—light and dark
unfolding through a tiny window—but even more
the fire of the fog's far edge, a smoldered haze
that is either a rare moment or a sign of the city's decay,

a sick red to make us grieve at the beauty
or exult—as Jeffers and Everson grieved, each
in their separate ways, exulting in how the light consumes
the dark, and the dark the light.

Fault Lines

When the rock seams
shear against each other
it is sometimes a small shrug—
like someone saying, "eh?"

Sometimes more a twitch.
Even one of those night
spasms when the whole body
jerks as if possessed.

Mostly it's as if someone
tugs our sleeve and we turn,
look into the eyes,
then pull away.

But each time the seams slip
we see the skin of grass
and pavement stretched across
the striated muscle of rock.

Each time we see that wholeness
is a history of dislocation
and want again a place to stand
as if we have stood there always.

Mackinaw Parade, 2004

First, notice the sky—the clouds
marching their own way, and the trees.
In small towns they are the skyscrapers.
But notice too the parade that draws us away
from clouds and trees. I like the green tractor,
shined up for show with the small boy
sitting in his grandfather's lap as if he too
will know the weather.

And also the flatbed trailer wrapped in blue
plastic with the women sitting up in white wicker,
each a red hat and red boa, slinky
against a blue dress. See the way they pose—
lifted shoulder and amused smile—offering
themselves for admiration. Theirs, they say, is not
a world of weather and no place is simple
unless we make it so.

(after Ken Kashian's photograph
"Mackinaw Parade, 2004")

Early Winter (Pacific Northwest)

Already the thin branches
are poking through
the sweater of stained leaves.

A few more nights of dark wind
and the bones beneath
will shine fully in the low sun.

Listening

There is a silence beneath the stories
where we learn the things that matter most.

It is like walking in a garden.
There are sculptures.

At first we see the objects, each
beautiful in turn—gray

curves of rock, the planes
of welded steel. Only later

do we begin to hear
the passing clouds.

Above Fort Collins (Summer, 1972)

So thin, he was like a whisper walking—
the white hair and stoop, the care of his step.
He no longer remembered, consciously,
how many landings there had been
or the nights before, nursing the cigarettes,
then bobbing toward the empty beach,
each as if alone in the floating shoebox of the LST.
Now only his body remembered the blood, slick
and gritty with sand, the viscera and disbelief—
the way the sound after the bullets tore him
was like looking through binoculars from the wrong end.
Even the lull of the morphine and pitching boat,
these too he had put away.

Now each morning he walked among the trees,
apple, pear, and plum, minding the rills of water
he'd teased from the creek that almost looped
the orchard and small frame house. The girl
who drove up the mountain sometimes
brought him things from town.
She thought he was alone. She didn't hear
the trees speaking to the wind, how they loved
the light, sometimes clear, sometimes tangled
in the dark clouds. She didn't hear
his hands as he looked across the range grass,
listening even to the ridges of rock.

2

Billboard
(Middletown, California, 1962)

At the edge of town the billboard map declares

MIDDLETOWN

Gateway to the Lake County Resorts

and the faded names—*Harbin's, Hobart's, Siegler's*
Hot Springs—cluster the painted lake
where a blonde woman skis in a shell of foam.
With one hand she waves to the road,
the other holds the rope from the boat
that must be in the scrub oak as it pulls her
across the water's peeled, white flecks.

Each summer, the tourists flow and ebb,
north to the lake resorts, then back
to the city. This is the gateway,
a place to pass through.
Here, where the rock buckles
into ravines of chaparral and the creeks
dry each summer to baked rock,
there is no reason to stop.

Passing through, the tourists do not see
the empty mines or the settlers from Missouri,
vaccinated with star thistle and trapped
like a steelhead that's crawled up the creek
whether there's water this spring or not.

Middletown

In late summer the sun
sharpens the star thistle
until the creek withers to its banks
like a pair of old gums.

In this heat each cricket whir
and whisper of the dried weeds
is the rattlesnake's blinded rustle,

and walking out from the small-roomed houses
you feel the brittle sheath tighten
until the blind eyes strain to cut
like teeth and strike the air.

Why the Land Is Red
(Lake County, California)

The old miners say
the cinnabar is why
the land is red,
but the ore is long smelted,
the retorts scrapped.

Now all that's left
are the bleached shacks
and the rust
of old bumpers.

The land must eat.

Lake County Elegy

When the dying was no longer slow enough,
the face emptied and the mask hissed to itself:
an old woman—and her children, themselves old,
and their children clustered about
as if the spoon bowl were still a hub.

I went outside and studied
not the oaks or hills
but my cousin's blocked-up and faded Model A,
loving it to a shine.

But like the rest I took an image: a brooch of hers
and his dress pocket knife, bone-handled, lint
and crust of deer gut on a blade honed
half away. Closed it and drifted.

Now like a child I sometimes dream
of the wagon trip west,
the days the houses were built, the mines worked.
But when we dance it is beer and neon, the slow
blossoming of rust on chipped chrome.
Soon the mottled skin will pock so thin
the wind will blow through.

Victrola

for my father

In that far room beyond the boxes
of things they'd not thrown away,
the Victrola stood higher than my head,
and when we'd visit I'd pick through
the brittle disks, black
beneath the dust and scratches,

wind the crank and climb on a smooth
stone to place the heavy arm
and listen to Campbell and Burr,
McCormack, Bing Crosby—the thin
scratch of the Irish songs floating
on the dusty shade and heat.

I didn't know, then, how the Victrola
had stood in the parlor when he was a boy
or how he had rested his hand on the oak's
darkened curve as if it were a grand piano.
I never saw him steady himself
to sing in a boy's clear voice, believing

in this Ireland of sound so different
from the rasp of the Grange dance fiddles.
Singing and singing to learn the notes,
he sang arias to his dream of being a voice
for all those who left him without the training
or anger to grab their throats and bless them, bless
them—the skip, skip, Caruso of the static.

Home Again

How saggy those springs must have been
if even then I slept rolled to the wall and twisted
as if uphill in the too-thin blanket
in that room with the torn wallpaper,
the bare bulb, the twirls of the cheap metal bed—
a visiting child's restless sleep.

But this is not
a poem. It is
the only voice I have
trying to say
those moments and this one
and the miles give me no room to play
because I do remember the hills

brown like the canvas worn through
the slipper's plush, and finding my way
through that dark house, the high walls leaking cold
by their very thinness, the oil heater's smell,
the wardrobes of sachet and dust—all of it
as strange and familiar as the old man's mouth without his teeth
as he looks up from his pillow and I stumble down the step
out to the toilet and the full night air.

To go back now would mean little. Too many are dead—
even that child this makes of my longing for the soft mouth
and the dark that hides the teeth at the bottom of the cup.

Star Thistle

In land this empty nothing grows well,
except the star thistle—thorns
so sharp they go right through your boot.

In the cemetery we work across the hillside,
checking the wooden markers against a chart
to find the plot she's chosen, then wait for the back-hoe
to stagger up the gully like a pallbearer too old for the work.

When the bucket's teeth grate through the stones and red dirt
splintering into old wood (so dry here it rots dusty),
we shovel as best we can to cover
those eyes of no reflection and make another hole.

At least the others will think she lies where she thinks
she lies, though the land means nothing to her now,
and we do not know what old man or woman
fed again on the mouthful of dirt
and wore the crown of star thistle.

The Web

The stories she wove
were nets of faint blood
hung with the beads

of old names. They were
like the web he'd found that morning.

It laced the white clapboard house
to the elderberry bush.
The shiny black husks

and bits of dew
glittered like glass.

1955

This was when the drive over the mountain
seemed forever, the car in second gear
leaning left, then right, then left again
up the switchbacks of slow trees,
the heat filling every eddy of shade.

This is the road to where the old people hug you
and you don't really mind and where the murmured
syllables you don't understand seem to mean
everything as the rocker's back and forth measures
the back and forth of their saying.

There are times I want to know those words
and what the saying meant as they rocked
back and forth from their different nows and thens.
I want to believe for that moment it was good
to be there, then. But other times what I want

is to wander away from the voices, down
the chipped cement steps to the different
shade of the black walnut, its emptier heat
of rock and thistle, the dirt redder than rust,
and be again alone in that way.

Lake County Diamond

Here the bits of quartz are "Lake County
Diamonds"—crystals washed down
from the high country where that flash
in a creek would mean a vein of ore
nearby: a drool of gold
twisting through a milky seam.

Drifting the shade of the creek,
we are searching for quartz chips
to decorate the wall that will separate
the house and oak from the dry weeds—
worthless crystals to embed
among the coins and scratched initials.

Gathering stones and old words,
we turn them in the water
to sluice away the crust of dirt.
They are diamonds
to scatter the light.

When the Back Steps
Seemed Very High

*for John who sees through the lens of his
camera and his brushes*

and Jessica who hears through the music she writes

It is late spring; even the mornings are already warm.
The tall door frames the table, the oilcloth
worn to the mesh where it drapes across the edge.
Across the kitchen, the pantry shelving is sculptural—
gray tones, black and white, and I can place,
if I try, the iron stove (beside the window you can't see
from here), the lard can and box of salt on the shelf,
even the tin ring for cutting biscuits, the feed store calendar.

But what matters are the chairs, the sagged cane
fixed with a pillow, and when you sat in them
they creaked and flexed as you leaned to the bowl of mush.
And the corner in the next room papered with greeting cards,
the light, brown through the shades drawn against the heat
as the rocking chair skreaks on the pine planks to the radio's
        slow waltz.
Holding the sag of his belly, his eyes closed, the old man
strolls arm in arm with the saxophones and violins
as if his life had been days and days of dancing.

These are things that fade or burn and die.
But in the afternoon light there is still the creak
of the freight wagons, the mules leaning into the long pull
up the mountain, and somewhere in the late winter light,
a harmonica plays in the corner after the day in the mine
as some write letters home and others watch
the notes drift with the snow.

This is part of why you walk down the street and still see
the bits of weed working through the cracks in the sidewalk
and why you hear how differently the air breathes
across the leaves of different trees. This is part of why
you know that things fade or burn and die
as they walk backward into the night.

Stories

For Irma Hunt Tarry, third child of eight (1912-1975)

As the cancerous thing grew in her mind
it took away the words
until she lived in her eyes.
Sometimes they looked out but mostly
she seemed searching inward
against the body's emptying space.

Perhaps she found those fields of lupine and poppy
above her grandfather's ranch and how each summer
the hills were waves of purple and orange
and the whole world seemed afternoon sun.

Perhaps she found the black walnut tree, the one
in front of the house in the town by the lake.
There was money for candy then.
It was where her brother died, the one who read books,
Tom Swift and His Motor-Cycle and *Tailspin Tommy*.
He strung the tree with copper wire, and through the crystal
in the box and the thing to her ear she heard voices
all the way from San Francisco, and faintly
a woman singing opera.

Still, he coughed himself to sleep.
They never knew why. Some said bad water
and they moved away. Then came the summers
living under the trees, across the creek
in that other town—a brass bed and wardrobe,
the pallets, night crickets, the owl.
And each morning the smoke of sidemeat
as the wood took fire in the stove.
Once her father told them he was "so starved

for their love" he would kill himself and that night
the sky beyond the branches opened to an immense black cell.

It was later that she schooled us—first her brothers
and sisters, then the rest as we came along—
reciting how her father charmed the rancher's daughter;
how they were married in Oakland the day after the '06 quake,
hand in hand while Frisco burned across the bay;
how—when the first son died—he had put away
the white shirts and red armbands and walked
away from the barbershop and soda fountain by the lake.

And then how the hard times came: driving wagon again
up from the valley where the train stopped
until the motor trucks came. Then, shoveling
the brown red cinnabar until mercury dropped
as if it too were a stock and the mines shut down.
Later came the days of no work—getting by
on out-of-season venison, the charity of store credit,
now and again a day on the county road crew.
And in her stories, always the rancher's daughter
learning to make do, brothers and sisters sticking together
as the sense of family grew rich as store bread
and so absolute that the marriages, when they came,
were not a going off but a coming home as each bride
put her ring in the cup over the kitchen's concrete sink.

This is how we learned that tricky pride
of the poor—the failing that is success.
How for a time we believed that true worth
is to matter only to each other.
The rootless trailers, the shuffled
and reshuffled marriages came later
as we grew into our different failings.
And as we learned things the stories did not say
she became silent and lived in her eyes.

Later, the others gave me bits she'd glossed
or erased. But it doesn't matter that her stories
were partly lies and mine now guesses. There were
flowers. I have seen that whole hillside
purple and yellow as if painted by the sun.
And there was a cup on the sill over the sink
where they put the gold rings
when they scrubbed the mismatched pots.
And the actual failures were always
there, each a grain of sand shelled within
the translucent tellings. And what else can we hold
when the cricket noise echoes at dusk
and the dust of the red dirt clings to the light
like the rust as the steam tractor burns
in the field behind the empty house. How else
do we face the ache of so much space
to fill with the human.

3

Listening to Art Tatum Play Piano

In this piece Tatum doesn't show off.
The right hand skips up the stairs
while the left shifts from foot to foot,
calling out as if unsure whether to follow
or turn back: a dialogue
improbable as a Hollywood romance—

street kid and sophisticate.
We know it won't work. It is only
in the script, but they have
found each other, and we do
see the angle of the cheekbone
and the way the eyes do hurt.

It doesn't matter it didn't happen. They
are on the steps. They have reached
the landing's almost alcove.
They are beyond the camera.
His hands rest on the keys.

Levi's 501s

One for the boys, one for the ladies,
he works at the mirror for hours
learning to sneer and smile
at the same time. And thank god
for Levi's with your hands in your pockets
and a roadhouse drawl—
'cause every country boy can sing
out a half his mouth, and baby
every town has a twobit Mason-Dixon
where us country boys dangle lines
from the ends of our Marlboros
'til it's back in the saddle again.

First Memory

1 (The Morning Call Café, New Orleans)

Here, even our faces are the color of worn wood
as we watch the three men in dingy smocks
shuffle back and forth bringing cups of chicoried coffee,
hot milk and the plates of beignets, the tiny
squares of fried dough, to roll in the powdery sugar.

As the sweet caffeine tangos the late-night wine,
we do our best not to see the way they walk
with the care of those who take no ground
for granted. We keep our eyes to the chalky countertop
and away from the mirrors front and back
that pitch the reflections in staggering echoes.

2

On the bench that raises him up in the barber's chair,
the teetering boy grips the enameled arms
where they have flaked like black dandruff.
The sheet tight about his throat, he stretches up
until the doubled mirrors of the cut-rate barbershop
catch the big ears and tiny head and he swims
against the reflections, trying not to laugh
with the scissors and cords, the thin-necked lotions.
He tries not to remember the high-piled boxes
of the new house and watching himself stare out,
for the first time an object among objects.

Driving

At sixteen I knew
each twist of the creek road
and just how much
the '57 Ford could
do through the curves.
I knew when
to brake going in
and how to pull through
to hit the bits of straight
where the road veered from the creek
into the light.

It was the going that mattered,
the beat of the radio,
clipping time, the tires
pulling against the turn—
being still within the road's
unreeling as if the car
was the world, as if I was
the world. And you,
in your different car,
knew this too,

driving fast but not
for the speed of it—
for the motion and how
the body's minute
calculations became
everything. As they again
become everything
as we slide through
different curves, driving
so perfectly that again

there is no world
but glass and speed.

Fishing

I cannot speak directly of
the wonderful mouth without words,
the dialogue of motion,
or the stillness that is also motion.
Such speaking empties the language
that we desire: the hands
describing soft places,
the slightly rough of the tongue,
the different slide of lips—
the words that are a shiny lure opening in the water
or the memory's lure mounted on some wall—
wonderful words wonderful mouths and breasts and thighs
and better that sweet almost painful reeling in,
the deep sea that is over and over
without lure or monument:
the dance that dies to dance
again and dies to yet more
still motion.

Shells

As these black marks edge right
to find a turning,
you are somewhere
beyond this white field.

In your time, the now
neatly blocked letters
march, pivot,
and march again

as the page smooths
your finger and you weigh
whether to turn away
or listen as if holding

a shell to your ear
for the way it magnifies
the blood's whispered pulse
into a sound like waves.

Inside the shell you offer your hand.
Our feet rise from the sand
above the whispering. See,
our dancing

is the music, is the weaving
this page into ours.

Peet's

At the Peet's in Berkeley, I am drinking a double
espresso with unrefined sugar in it; you, a mocha.
Do you remember in high school how we'd walk
the campus, prowl the bookshops, then sit here as if
this were more real than the little town to the north—
the apple trees and canneries, evenings
of *Rawhide, Lawrence Welk, Route 66*?

No, you don't. Because I am not in Peet's.
Here, no one else is up yet. I am drinking tea
(from the Peet's in Portland) as the blue
squeezes down against the fog, and the trees
come out across the estuary.
And you? I don't know who you are
as I write pretending I do.

But if you were you and we were sitting in Peet's, each
detail would draw another. "Do you remember
when?" "And how we . . . ?" "And that time . . ." until
we could put on the world we'd woven
and stare off through that window at what might pass by.

Or, to remember differently. It is Sunday evening,
a small college town in Maine. The control panel's meters
cast puddles of light on the spinning vinyl
feeding Ellington to all the someones who might hear
if they happened to turn their radio dials that way.
Is anyone there? Or am I alone with the Duke and Johnny Hodges
talking to myself between numbers as I pretend
to talk to you and you and you, each in your separate
living rooms, where the light is different in each.

Here, this morning, the air is still cool, it lifts
off the water as the light grows within it
and you draw the ink across the page.
Perhaps where you are the light is also
warming your skin. Perhaps
as we share the passing by
these words are not silence.

Language

It is not the letters
marching
the matted white
of the page
in starched
black uniforms
as they try
to blend
the blatty
consonants
and reedy vowels
into more
than sound.

Rather, it is
the tongue's
motion, the hand
riding the waves
as they spill
up the beach,
then lace out
into the sand
leaving behind
the broken
bits of shell
that mark the tide.

Eucalyptus

for Nancy Rouke Hunt, 1930-1995

1

Months ago I sat beside her, the winter light
low through the window as if warm.
That we grow old and die is beyond sense
until it begins to come for us, not with a certain date
but that vague soon, soon enough, too soon . . .
and it comes to seem all there is.

But that day there were memories—
perhaps from the fear but almost
covering it as a fall of snow mutes
the hillside's litter of rocks and blown branches.

Some stories we tell to know who we are,
who we think we are, as we walk the same paths
over and over, until the dirt packs
and the weeds no longer grow.

This time as she talked she strayed
into the clump of trees—the eucalyptus
so slender they sway in even the slightest wind—
surprised at the things not in the stories.

There are paths in the trees but not the ones
we've made, and the long, thin leaves play the light
across the shadows that smell like bay.
This day she talks as if she could stay

where she has wandered, in the trees,
beyond the path and the hillside
that waits for the shawl of snow.

2

The last night there were flickerings of almost lucidity
when she seemed still to know us, but dimly
through the morphine—like a child
still learning the simple weave of things.
Through the hours, I sat beside her, reading.
She did not follow the story or see the pictures
from the words, but she heard through the dream
the syllables pacing the frame of the page.

Somehow, it mattered to be there, waiting
for the almost recognitions. It mattered
that there be a yes to answer the eyes.

Soft Shoe

I am dancing again the Grapevine, my feet
weaving left over right, right behind left,
whisking the floor like brushes on a snare drum.

My grandfather taught me this step.
Smiling through my missing teeth
and squeaky voice, I waved the red,

white and blue cane as his fingers
searched the chipped keys for the chords
and my feet stumbled for the pattern.

Now, there are no showy colors as I work
across the stage and back again, chirping
the vaudeville words—"June" and "moon"

and "spoon"—marking each step with a stab
of the cane as my feet whisper the varnished wood,
left over right, right behind left.

Beyond the footlights your faces are a black pool.
Some of you read the program by the exit light.
Others follow the spotlight back and forth

as if I glow . . . and matter. But what matters
is the placing of the feet, singing—hearing—
as if "June" and "moon" and "spoon" were

revelation. What matters is the envelope the spot
makes through the darkness we share and the light
we share. In this seam my feet trace across the wax

as if smoothing the scarred wood, left over right,
right over left, whisking the floor, keeping time.

The Summer She Was Seventeen (1947)

In the cannery the women in long rows sit on stools
coring, peeling apple after apple, each one
picked from the cold sluice of water,
then placed for the spinning blades: lean
and reach, lean and reach, as the sun climbs the tin wall,
naps on the roof through midday, and so slowly
backs down the far wall to quitting time.

                                                 All day
the women around her talk as the ache builds
first in the fingers, then the shoulders and settles
in the small of the back. They talk of hurried meals,
husbands and lovers, the scrimping and moments
of pleasure that ache within the dark
of the brief summer nights as the cannery's stink
cools toward another morning.

Reaching, reaching again into the cold water
she hears the shards of fear that glint through the cracks
in the stories, the bitterness, and too those bits of pleasure
that play within the tin walls of must and ought
like the motes of light in the high shadows
as the sun climbs, rests, and crawls
back down all summer, day after day.

Night Shift, First Death
(Children's Hospital, Seattle)

for Susan

The child should not have lived—can not.
Someone wheels it to an empty room.
The parents do not come
and perhaps it's best

but you cannot bear her to die
alone, though she cannot know
she is alone and dying.
And for hours after the night of work
you rock to the slow stilling
in an empty room.

You do not see the light
grow around the curtain.
You do not hear your singing,
until you stop as if wondering

why you are there
without a name or past—
a slat of glare
where the curtains do not meet.

I do not pretend to understand
the lullaby of death as you turn
in this dark and become hers again
and we wait to see what light will come.

"We need to talk . . ."

Let us imagine that we are beside a creek.
The water pools as if it is still.
Looking out, each with our carefully
gathered stones—the smooth ones, flat, rounded,
we skip them across the surface.
Each touch of the stone is another kiss
deflecting from the moments of water.

It is all in the angle of the hand,
the stone spinning off the end of the finger.
We have become so good at this we
no longer think about it. The stone comes
into the hand, the arm arcs, and we are talking
on this surface of water, your stone, then mine,
yours again across the late morning.

The Last Patrol

for Verdon "Spur" Spurlock, 1916-1999

In the dark beyond the window
the channel's deep current and incoming tide
are a diagonal of riffled water. It is there
below the one tree where the eagle
sometimes pauses from his fishing.
Even this late there are a few lights along the far shore—
the scatter of houses where someone cannot sleep,
the blinking refinery that by day
is a thicket against the stretch of the mud flats.

You have never forgotten the desert stars beyond
the campfire's ebbing, the dark tang of the horses,
and clumps of sage after the day's long ride. You were,
then, a boy in a company of men masquerading as men,
and so a man. That was before the long march—
the hills of Italy, France, Korea's frozen mud, patrol
after patrol of the boys who were men and too often
the flicker in the eyes asking belief as the dark spread out
to the fingertips you held as firmly as you could.

Tonight in the chair that faces the window
you walk a different patrol—not through death
but with it, as the pain bursts like a shell, then ebbs
to the fingertips with the turning tide.
It is not easy to refuse the delay of tubes and needles,
to turn away from the slow rot, to not call out,
to die alone, but tonight the stars above the tide are
desert stars, they are fireflies flickering in the trees.
Through the glass you cannot hear the slide of wings
as the owl's shadow blinks across the tiny points of light.

Play Stove

for Jessica

A story is a kind of knitting:
the hooked needles tie the dyed strands
into a cloth that divides warm from cold.
The story does not do this—the telling—a spell
we cast on ourselves through the one who listens.
I will tell you a story.

The play stove from when you were little
is in the cellar. Your grandfather and I made it
that winter we lived on the ranch far from town.
We cut it down from an old hi-fi cabinet
from the dump behind the cottonwoods
and scavenged the knobs and burners,
the enameled back plate. Your grandfather's hands
were twisted, arthritic. We worked in the shed
when there were bits of sun.

You were too young to want a stove, and we could
have driven to town—K-Mart—for one of the new
plastic ones with the big numbers on the dials.
But in this story I am the saw and hammer
and he is making something better than store-bought.
He knows that by the time you play with the stove
you will not think about its making,
but he is making it for you.
If he were here, I do not know what story
he would tell. This is the one I tell.

4

Passing Through (Nevada Night)

At 4 a.m. in one of those casinos in a town that isn't,
we are two college boys stopping for coffee and still
hoping to make the salt flats by dawn.
The waitress, too tired to look as hard as she is,
watches a last drunk spoon quarters to the slot machine
as if feeding cereal to a child.

Outside, the air is almost cool, the day's heat echoing
from the sidewalk and one paved street—the coffee,
a momentary pledge against the next stretch of road,
no more real than the false fronts hung on the buildings, no less
than the trailers that straggle down the dirt side street.

A college boy, I stood wondering why she didn't leave
and seemed to know that one of those trailers
held a child and little else. And after all the years,
this is what comes back—not the miles
and hours of the old VW or the moon seemingly bright

or the dawn glare off the salt shattering across the windshield,
but this place: no voices and each object desert sharp,
a bit of tree between dirt and moon—this,
the place of getting by.

Car Radio When It Seemed Late at Night (Gunsmoke)

Do you remember the drive home
after the long day of visiting
and how the tree branches
would wipe away the stars,
then give them back as you watched
through the back window
and the car swayed to the road
that worked along the creek
and through the gap in the hills.

After the many minutes that seem much longer,
the faint clicking of the tappets,
the space between your parents,
and the humming tires are a silence.
All you hear is the radio.
Marshal Dillon is talking to Miss Kitty.
You do not know yet the word "madam"
or "whore." You do not know what you hear

in their voices or how to name
the silences in the front,
but what you hear is more than "madam"
or "whore" and you trust it, believe it,
even though you are nowhere in it,
as you listen to the layering of voices
and the faint smear of stars appears
and disappears again and again
in the oval of the window.

Fleeing a Dust Storm: 1936
(Cimarron County, Oklahoma)

Farm Security Administration Documentary Photograph

The man shields
the camera's eye
to frame a moment.
The lens opens.
An instant
burns through
and the shutter's
blades harvest
the scraped
swaths of light
onto the field
of the glass plate:

In this gray window, we see the dry wind,
shallow roots—the snagged tumbleweeds
singing in the barb wire as the fence posts sink
in the drifts of dust.

We see the man and boy, shielding their faces
from the stinging grit. They lean
as if swimming upstream
for the gray shack on the far shore.

We do not see what is in the shack
or next month or the year after—but
this moment as if there was, then,
only loss and grief to go with the love.

Absence (Sebastopol, California)

1. (Lloyd Phillips Rouke, 1905-1984)

On the gray screen two black men all but naked
weave in and out, working the body, working a cut above the eye.
Each time the bell rings a cartoon parrot flitters across—
the Gillette jingle. It is Friday, the fights: the quick hands
and careful shuffling feet, the announcer's spiel.

Elbows on knees, my grandfather breathes in another Camel.
He is intent, elsewhere, as I sit and do not even think
to ask the how or why of that gray dance—
watching as he stares out just beyond
the stained fingers and flaring ember.

2. (Grace Wilson Rouke, 1911-1963)

In that kitchen with the cheap linoleum and chairs that didn't
        match
she was still almost young—
a little harsh around the rouge and cigarettes, a look
I now see as from the war years.

The heart attack that dropped her to the floor was mercifully quick
and she disappeared from our lives.

But death is not a disappearing. It is an arresting, a putting
away of the unresolved and never known—a gap
so dense it bends the light and the way we walk
long after we have forgotten the brand of the cigarettes,
the putting away—even the absence.

Plate Glass (Sebastopol, California)

(On finding that the house
my grandfather built had burned)

Through the fence, I can see the apple trees
that were once an orchard,
but where the house would be
a steel water tower hovers like a green rock.
It feeds the new houses that have crept out from town,
where people read *Sunset* and *California Living*,
admire the twisted trees through their plate glass,
and drive quiet cars to the cubicles we now call work.

This is not a bad life: the morning light
combing the fog from the trees,
the clouds redeeming the day just at twilight.
And no one leans out from the tall ladders,
arms growing heavy as the limbs grow light.
No one kneels in the soft dirt for the fallen
apples, bucket after bucket, breathing the dust
until the mouth tastes of mud. And even
when the air is right on the summer nights, the mash
from the cider presses no longer leaches
rotting apples through every closed window.

But even when this hill was still outside of town,
the trees were too old to pay off—just another 1930s
dream of getting ahead, getting free
of the scramble to please for less and less
against the monthly rent, the hair thinning in the mirror,
the distance across the table at night.

That first fall when he moved them from the city,
he built a square room of grayed planks, a tar paper roof,
windows on two sides. All winter he hired out as he could—
working on the kitchen when the rain and light allowed:
narrow, with a window watching the cleared space
to where the hilltop fell in steep scrub.

A whole winter they lived in that room missing the city,
not missing it, finding ways to be apart, just as the cold
leaking through the planks found the seams
within the heat from the woodstove in the corner.

Later, that room was a tangle of chairs, vacuum hoses,
boxes of jars, and books the mice had been at.
The house was then an L of chalky shingles
with geraniums growing in skinny tires
next to the abalone shells that lined the dirt walk
through the weeds and grass.
In the morning fog they were gray and silver,
in the afternoon they glowed like tiny sunsets.

If I climbed the fence, the ruts to the house
would still be there, and maybe bits of shell and shingle.
Instead, I turn to my wife and children waiting by the car,
"Over there, that's where they lived." And I want to say,
The shallow well tasted of rust, she wore rouge
and lipstick bright against her fading hair
and even then the space between them
was like the space between the kitchen's cheap linoleum
and the shed of littered tools from the failed schemes.
I want to say in winter the weeds behind the kitchen
were a green flame as if summer could burn again.

Driving My Father Home
After Visiting His Sisters

1

Out here where the road starts up the mountain
there are still no houses, and looking beyond the car window
my father talks of how he would walk from town
into these hills—the scattered thickets of oak
and manzanita. In his voice the world is still
brittle leaves underfoot, a hawk over the next
hilltop, the lean of the gun barrel against his thigh
as he rests under a tree and the dog pants against the heat.

In all my imaginings I never saw him walking this far
beyond the nets of oughts and mustn'ts. Here.
In the tone of his words it's as if the boy
already sensed how the sun walking across the day
would become no longer enough, then slowly
become nearly enough again.

2

Someday, you will be the one driving the car
guessing at what is the same, and different,
reaching for the details the stories never hold.
I am, what, seven, eight? Riding a tiny bike to a new school.
The street is still shadow even as the light crests over the roofs
and shines against the windows on the right. The houses
are tall rocks. Perhaps this morning
I will make it to the top without stopping.
Or a few years later, a different house, another school,

the long walk down the orchard to crawl through the wire fence,
then across the cow field as the light pushes
the fog off the far hill. I can remember the grass,
dark green from the fall rains, the mist
from my mouth, even that sense of being suspended
in a space that was not ordinary, but mostly that it was far.

Queen for a Day

Winter. 1959. Dion is still "A Teenager
in Love" and every day at noon
my mother and I watch *Queen for a Day*
with Campbell's Tomato Soup
and tuna fish on Wonder Bread.

We never wondered if the stories were true.
I think they were—the wives and mothers
with crippled children, absent husbands,
and unpaid bills: each reciting her need
and how she bore up under the luck
that placed her there to be brave and needy
instead of watching her make us believe.

And then came the wonderful moment
when we all clapped to choose our Queen for a Day
and she was led to her throne, robed and crowned,
roses and scepter laid in her lap and that announcer,
the one with the *My Man Godfrey* moustache,
read the gifts she had bought with our belief:
a refrigerator for the baby's milk, wheelchair, a car
that ran, and always a something nice for her
as the camera held the tearful smile.

Each day we watched, like all the others
in the two-bedroom bungalows—the fenced
squares of lawn mowed with those mowers
with the curved blades that whirred as you pushed,
the washer/dryer on the porch, a Ford
that used a little oil but ran. Each day
we clapped. Each day we believed.

Canned Tuna

In the photo he is seven or eight.
Twine cinches his pants to his waist.
Hair slicked back, he is smiling
as if he wants the camera to like him
but isn't sure it will. I do not know
whether this was before or after
he smoked his grandfather's cigars
behind the oak tree and thought
no one knew why he was sick and pale.

So little, they called him flea, and every time
they sent him to the butcher shop he got pork chops
no matter what he'd been told to get—so they called him
pork chop, too. And the clothes came down
brother to sister to brother and each year
a pair of catalog shoes that sometimes fit.

Does it matter that canned salmon was cheap
when he was a boy? It was what you ate, night after night
when the butcher cut off credit but the grocer
kept you going—that, beans, out-of-season venison,
whatever was left from the summer canning.

Such differences are obvious, but they were then
as much the ordinary as the canned tuna on toast
the end of the month when I was a boy—not signs
of making do. What was. That's the trick—to read
what was.

Algebraic Topology

1

Pretend you are holding the end of a string.
Taut, vibrating. A few inches below your thumb
and forefinger it disappears into a rock
or hillside—some place you cannot follow.
In theory we could read these vibrations to know
the string's length, the knots that thicken it,
even the rock we cannot see. This would be like
converting waves of sound into strings of numbers,
then back again to hear the image of a voice from a radio.
Listen. The vibrations are singing granite and shale,
layers of sand, water, even milky quartz, the seams
black in the absence of light.

2

The ashtray next to the piano is a brass sombrero,
the brim a circle of ash and butts.
On the sheet music slim silhouettes
in evening gowns and top hats
sway as if in wealthy nonchalance.

The man is playing "Darktown Strutters Ball."
The boy in the straightback chair watches
the browned fingers moving
across the stained ivory of the keys

and listens as he sings "I'll be down to get you
in a taxi, honey." She "better be ready by half past
eight . . .not late." He wants to be there when
"the band starts playing." I know he does,

though he sings as if the words don't matter, as if
he is sharing only the music—a two-step that he plays
in ragged syncopation more vaudeville than jazz
in the way the harmony clothes the blue notes
in tails and evening gowns.

Visiting

for Ellis "Dutch" Hunt

1

The night you showed me how to pick the note,
then chord, alternating root and fifth in the base,
I was eight? nine? It was Main Street, the house
next to the liquor store where the train tracks
ran down the middle of the street and the cars
edged toward the curb when the train crept through.

The lamplight was a circle around you as you sang
"Red River Valley," "You Are My Sunshine,"
"Keep on the Sunny Side." I think I sang too,
as your fingers walked from G to C to D
and back again, showing the pathways
through the grid of string and frets.

2

Today, the noon sun steps
through the front window
and leans against the far wall
as you sing with my children.

After, the guitar rests in the open case,
the rosewood a darker light,
as we watch the sun gape and stretch.
Soon, we will drive down from the hills,

back across the valley. The light
will walk along behind us, then step beyond
to slip into the water at the ocean's far edge,
burning the clouds, the coals glowing
rosewood, then gray, then black.

The Day After the 100th Anniversary of the '06 San Francisco Quake

Let us anchor a now—like driving a spike into the rock
to mark a place. It is summer, 2006. The glaciers
are melting. The Middle East is a tapestry of faith and flame.
Each night the news is bleeding children and the haze
of words that pretend to be more real. This is part of now.

Another part: I am 56, our children are finding
their different ways. I do not have a cell phone.
I do not have an iPod. I still ink marks onto a page
then type onto a screen. Sometimes I ride a bicycle to work.
Somehow we have stayed whole, or rather become so.

Here is another. The Grange Hall, Middletown, California,
1956—my grandparents' fiftieth wedding anniversary.
Someone has sent a picture. We are all lined up—
aunts and uncles and cousins. I am the youngest,
smiling in a little jacket and tie as if I belong.

The "Ring Bear," I stood beside my grandfather.
Someone made my grandmother a golden dress.
It was after that the man lined us in front of this gray wall,
then stood on a stool with his head under a black cloth.
We are all, carefully, within the moment,

except my grandmother—smiling, as if remembering
the day they were married, Oakland, 1906 and walking out
from the courthouse the day after the quake,
the smoke so dark across the Bay it seemed the sun
must have gone east.

There is a gulf between these different nows, but
also a cabling that loops from one spike to another
as if suspending a bridge across the fall
to the channel and the tide's motion.
Looking down, the lights reflect from the water.

Pentagon March
(Washington, DC, 1967)

(Seen in a Time of War, Fall 2007)

I have seen the pictures—the mass of us
shuffling across the causeway in ragged rows.
In the clips they show now boys with beards
raise their fists, and there are signs with slogans.
We are angry, the clips say, this is a protest.
The clips say this is where things changed:
Kent State, Catonsville Nine, Chicago Seven,
SDS, Symbionese Liberation Army, Nixon
resigning, Black Panthers, Dope, Sex,
and Rock 'n' Roll. But the clips
were not there, the clips do not remember.

I have forgotten the name of the boy
whose car we drove, but it was a Saab,
rusty, and the motor so tiny that each time
you filled up you mixed the oil and gas
straight into the tank like an old lawn mower,
and on the hills you coasted down for the speed,
then slowed with the climb to the next hilltop.

All night we drove through the Adirondacks
and when the sun rose and we turned south
onto the freeway, we were a river, cars and buses
flowing past eddied convoys of Army trucks,
soldiers hunched in the backs.
They stared out as we slid past. It was
easier to look at the faces in the cars
and buses, and sometimes we waved.
Mostly we were quiet, thinking of the soldiers

and why there were so many. Perhaps
they worried too.

I do not remember where we left the car
or finding the Reflection Pool, to crowd in
and wait, but I remember walking slowly
across the causeway, the sense of doing
something that must be done—
that we were asking Why and trying to say
No, as we watched the cameras
that watched us walk, and I remember now
that our walking was a kind of grieving,
not for the soldiers, as it should have been,
but for ourselves, our sadness at the idea
of the skin of flame enwrapping the lives
that seemed simpler than our own,
and our sense that we could not bear
to live so simply. But as we walked,
we did believe it would end.

Still Life with Voice and Music

1 (CBS Evening News)

When I would watch my parents
watching the news, it was always
Cronkite intoning from the gray screen.
Once Khrushchev was banging his shoe,
once people reeled in streams of water
and big dogs snarled at their leashes;
sometimes there were pictures of a pluming
cloud, once men clung to a wire fence,
the thin bones glowing through the rags
like X-rays or cartoon skeletons. I know now
that this last was not the news, only a document.
I know now that these things were called Freedom
Riders, McCarthy Hearings, Nuclear Winter, Cold War,
fear and desire to live and be decent, fear and
"Father Knows Best," fear and all this makes
no sense but someone is telling us it does.
And each night as Cronkite intoned from the gray
screen, the no sense and the someones telling
us it does walked hand in hand.

2 (October 1962, Waiting)

In the school hallway
the doorway light
scuffs the gray tiles.

We hug our knees
lined to the wall.
We are very quiet.

3. (Marin County, California)

It was spring 1966 and late enough that the days
were sometimes sunny, as this one was.
It was the game where Kenny let the ground ball roll
straight through his legs at third and didn't even see it
because he was watching the girl whose pants were so tight
it seemed you could see everything we wanted as she walked
back to the stands holding a coke and we all laughed at him.
Even Kenny laughed. And after, we waited on the grass
in front of that school where the rich kids went.
A transistor radio played "Turn Turn Turn," the Byrds,
the twelve-string chiming, and two girls in granny dresses
with long hair and Franklin glasses, like McGuinn's,
danced and the sun danced. They were splashes of color
as if the world were new, forever, and we were
so giddy in their spinning, our spinning,
we did not hear our prayer.

Postscript (Threads)

Take a thread of cotton,
of creek or of blood,
it doesn't matter. We are
like children
threading a needle
to stitch carefully
through the very
tips of our fingers
to dance hand
to hand, weaving
an unraveling cloth
of touch.

About the Poet

A fourth-generation native of Northern California, Tim Hunt was born in Calistoga and raised primarily in Sebastopol, two small towns north of San Francisco. At that time, Sebastopol was still primarily apple orchards, and the wine industry had not yet made Calistoga chic. As a boy he also identified strongly with the Lake County region of his father's family, an area where quicksilver mining had once been profitable.

Educated at Cornell University, he has taught American literature at several schools, including Washington State University and Deep Springs College. He is currently Professor of English at Illinois State University, in Normal, Illinois. He and his wife, Susan, a respiratory therapist, have two children: John, a visual artist, and Jessica, a musician and composer. Hunt once claimed to have been the rhythm guitarist in the band Derridean Debris, though to the best of his knowledge such a band never existed.

Hunt's poetry has been widely published in magazines, and he has published the chapbook *Lake County Diamond*. He has also been awarded the Chester H. Jones Prize for the poem "Lake County Elegy." *Fault Lines* is his first full-length collection. His scholarly publications include *Kerouac's Crooked Road: Development of a Fiction* and the five-volume edition *The Collected Poetry of Robinson Jeffers*. The URL for Tim Hunt's website is: www.tahunt.com.

Breinigsville, PA USA
19 January 2010
230984BV00003B/4/P